My marriage is almost dead

and my husband doesn't get it

CAROLYN KLASSEN

ISBN: 978-1-7751751-1-7

DEDICATION

To my husband. Jim puts in deliberate effort every day to keep our marriage alive and vital. While books and teachers and colleagues have taught me about marriage, my husband gives me the incredible experience to have me feel what an engaged and loving husband feels like--every day.

CONTENTS

ACKNOWLEDGMENTS

To the clients who have taught me about relationships, courage, fear and vulnerability. Counseling school taught me some. You taught me much more. Even as we were exploring your story, your questions, your pain, your relationships, and your journey, I was learning from you. I am grateful.

Carolyn Klassen

Prologue

I've been a therapist for a lot of years. I work with men, women, and couples. So often, even when I work with individuals, I hear that people are doing the best they can, but it falls short of being able to meaningfully connect in the most important relationship in their lives: their marriage.

We are raised in ways, as boys and girls, in our Western world that make marriages difficult. It might be the twenty first century, but gender stereotypes persist. Women are acculturated to be quiet, cooperative and "nice". Men are told to be tough, work hard, and not let people see them tender. When people get locked into who our culture tells them to be, it takes away from being who they really are. It takes away from being able to authentically connect.

It makes it harder to have a vital and enriching marriage that is good for both partners.

May the pages you read inside this book challenge some of those patterns that you and your partner may have been stuck in. May these pages open doors to tender conversations that can start to bring back some of the closeness you both want. May reading spur challenging but good conversations that will get you, as a couple, into a therapist's office where you can both do the hard work of finding your way back to each other.

As a therapist, I'm all about better relationships. I'm all about helping people in my office, through the written word, and in the seminars and workshops I deliver to connect better with each other. The hardest relationships are generally the ones that are the most important. Marriage is a super important relationship. Divorce is painful for the couple, their children, family, and friends.

However, as a therapist, I am not about saving marriages at all cost.

This book is not intended to minimize abuse of any kind. This book is not encouraging you to stay in an unsafe home. Or intended to have women who have been made to feel small in their lives feel any smaller. This is about strengthening and empowering you as a woman to speak truth in a way your husband will hear it. If you have been beaten down, physically and/or mentally and/or emotionally, know that you may need extra help to feel empowered. No one deserves to be hurt—and that includes you. Please ensure that you are safe. Don't use this book to feel worse about yourself, please.

Now—on to finding words and language to understand how you feel, which will shape how you talk, which will impact on your behaviors and actions, which will shape your life. May your life be shaped positively because of your time spent pondering these pages.

1 BE REAL. "NICE" DOESN'T WORK FOR ANYBODY

It breaks my heart when women are so nice that they don't tell their partners or their friends or their kids when they are mad. When women are hurting, or feeling ignored or upset, or things just aren't working, culture often dictates that they swallow their discomfort.

It frustrates me when women:

- suppress what they want to have happen
- pretend it didn't really hurt all that much
- or stop themselves from expressing a different opinion on the matter

It particularly drives me a little crazy when women are doing all of these nice things for the sake of the relationship.

- Isn't it nice to let him choose pizza without mentioning you'd really prefer sushi? Isn't it the "right thing" to give in when he says he wants pizza without working out a collaborative solution for how to make it work for both of you?

- Isn't it kind to pick up his socks over and over without saying anything? Or if you do say something, and he doesn't listen, then giving up and just doing it anyway?
- Isn't it polite to not belabor how painful it was at the party when he got drunk and was so rude to your friends? Not bringing it up the next day makes the whole day go so much easier!
- Doesn't it help the relationship to "suck it up" when he trivializes the promotion you got at work, and goes on as if it doesn't matter? After all, women are supposed to not need the encouragement of their spouses these days (or so goes the feminist line, anyway).

What breaks my heart is that well intentioned, beautiful, sensitive, caring women live the above, while:

- swallowing hurts
- pretending they don't have preferences
- ignoring their own sensitivities
- trying their darndest to express them so caringly to the other...that they end up dismissed/ignored or simply not heard at all

What frustrates me is that months and years and decades of suppressing their own preferences and ideas, being hurt repeatedly without any change on behalf of the other, well, it *wears on a woman*. That then *wears on the relationship*, and the rope of connection becomes increasingly frayed...

...more and more...

until, one day...

it snaps.

And. She's. Done.

And that is often when the guy phones our office for an appointment and says, "My wife says she's leaving. I knew she wasn't thrilled, but I had no idea it was as bad as this, and I want to do something. I love her and I want her, and I'll do anything to change. Help me. I'm desperate to save this marriage."

And it's too late. She really is done.

All that "niceness" builds up resentment and pain and distance. In the end, **"niceness"**—the suppression of good old honest anger that could clear up the little nigglings which are inevitable in all relationships—**contributes to the demise of the relationship**.

For many women, the idea of actively expressing anger as a way of building relationship, and enhancing connection is something that seems a little crazy. The thought of making your spouse profoundly uncomfortable by being bold about what's not working for you can seem absurd. For many women, actively teaching your husband how to be a husband to you, with your dreams and plans, your styles and quirks seems counterintuitive to being a good wife.

But it's not.

Expressing clearly and effectively what isn't working is a gift you give your spouse…because when it isn't working for you, it isn't working for anybody.

When it works for you and your spouse **both**, *then* it is working for everybody. Let this book have you think through how to talk to your spouse about your discomfort in your marriage.

Some chapters won't apply to your situation—no need to read those. Grab ideas of how to communicate. Remember phrases that say what you feel in ways you've never been able to articulate. Highlight portions that speak your heart, your pain, your dreams. Know that this book is to be used in whatever way is helpful for you to have a better relationship.

This book isn't therapy, nor is it intended to replace therapy. It's maybe a bit of "pre-therapy"—it is a chance to be real with yourselves and each other about the *state of your union*. Once you are honest with yourselves and each other, then you can figure out a plan.

I believe in couple therapy. Of course I do. I do couple therapy with couples and I see it work. I see couples get stronger, figure things out, reconnect with each other, find their first love. For many of you, that might be the way to go.

Couple therapy isn't cheap, but it is priceless!

Find a way that works for the two of you, with your own quirks and interests and style. But make sure it works for both of you. Keep at it, try different things until something works.

2 IF IT AIN'T WORKIN' FOR BOTH OF YOU, IT AIN'T WORKIN'

Dear Wives-who-are-lonely,

This is a horrifying statistic: 69 percent of divorces are initiated by women. [i]

Over 2/3's of divorces occur because the wives say, "Enough".

I want husbands to have a chance to learn that it isn't working before it's too late. As a marriage therapist, I've met very few husbands who don't care about their wives, and *intentionally* ignore their relationship. As a matter of fact, so many husbands seem to be gob smacked when their wives tell them they are done.

Wives, you didn't get married expecting it to end. I know you had dreams and hopes about the future.

And somewhere, things went sideways.

You're likely tired, and frustrated. And I'm sorry that it feels exhausting and demoralizing to be living the life you are in.

If you're the typical wife, you do an hour more of housework per day than your husband.[ii] You spend double the amount of time caring for others than he does. It's not easy to do so much of the heavy lifting around the house.

First of all, being responsible for so much is just plain hard. Maybe you also work full time. But even more than that, the difference in workloads is just plain unjust. It's hard not to be resentful when he's tired and relaxing in front of the TV, and you're tired and making lunches for the next day.

I know you are doing the best you can. If you're like most women, you've been taught that a good woman doesn't complain, she just does what it takes to make everything work.

When he needs extra time at work, you pick up the slack. When he has a chance to get away with the guys and tells you he needs a break, you just take on single parenting duties without missing a beat. When the playoffs are on, you work to fill the house with snacks for him and his friends. You work really hard to be supportive of him. As Dr. Gottman would say, you accept influence from your husband very naturally.[iii]

When you have a business trip, you leave notes about what everybody needs to do and when.

If you are out to book club for the evening, you paste on a frozen grin when your mother says, "Isn't it nice he *babysits* so you can go out?" Because you know, you raise the children, and he babysits. (NOT!!) Your mother intends to support you, and she wants you to have your own time, but she isn't even aware of her language.

And you recognize that given the pace of the family, it doesn't make sense to apply for a promotion at work. (Even though neither of you would think to have him slow his progress up the ladder at his employment.)

Wife-who-feels-ignored…can I tell you something that is honest, but maybe hard for you to believe?

The husband in your life doesn't get it. He genuinely doesn't.

If you ask him, he will likely say he does half-the-work-of-the-household-*ish*. He doesn't know how much more you do that he isn't even aware. He also sees you generally cheerful and mostly cooperative as you go about doing so much—which is true, because you like making a home for your family. You wouldn't dream of guilting your kids or your mother for what you do for them, right?

***

I think the husbands of this world don't recognize that their marriages are slowing dying.

You are disappearing from your marriage slowly, drop by drop, and your husband doesn't even notice.

You may have just found your eyes suddenly start to leak. You teared up just now because you feel, at last, understood. This marriage isn't life-giving like you dreamed it would be…as your husband believes it still is.

In my experience as a therapist, women are often much unhappier in the marriage than the husband realizes. Often she comes to therapy alone, desperate to change something—and her husband will not come to therapy for any number of excuses which all boil down to one reason: he doesn't want to come to therapy.

To be fair, therapy involves talking about feelings, something that men are raised to believe is not something that they are good at. And actually, some men *really aren't* good at it. How many of us can do anything well if we have never done it before, and no one ever modelled it for us or showed us how? Men are raised in a culture that says people who go to therapy to talk about feelings are wusses or sissies.

And what are men called who go to therapy because their wives ask them to? Well, there are several names for those sorts of men. None of them positive.

So…you're dying inside as you live in a marriage that looks pretty good from the outside: you're paying down the mortgage, going on a vacation with the kids, putting money into RRSP's and maybe going out for dinner on Friday night. It all looks pretty good.

Except it ain't workin' for you—and it hasn't for a long time.

I have had clients who were wives that were wonderful women quite willing and ready to overfunction as a sign of their love for the first several years of their marriage. Young brides can be cheerfully dismissive how he goes off with the boys, buys big ticket items for his own leisure with joint funds, and forgets to put his dishes away etc. etc. Most wives can do that for a decade or so. But when the kids come along, and the amount of work goes up exponentially, his disregard for her disproportionate efforts stops being cute and gets annoying. But he's used to underfunctioning and doesn't understand how serious it is.

Dear-wives-who-are-being-ignored, this isn't nearly all about housework either, is it? This is about the life partner who promised to support you, now:

- tunes you out while he plays video games
- plans his weekend and then has you plan around his plans
- is not aware of how tired you are
- does not check in with you about your day, or what you would choose as the family's next big project to save for, or maybe just about doesn't check in with you at all

And, wives-who-are-lonely, some of you are so discouraged, that you are putting in time until the kids are older, or are already planning your exit—and he doesn't know it.

I get it.

You were raised in a culture that said *nice* women work hard and don't complain.

No one wants to be a "witch with a b". Women are used to being the one responsible for resolving the conflict, and maintaining the wellbeing of the relationship in the majority of relationships.

So, women keep the peace in a relationship that isn't working well for them by:

- speaking up…but not too loudly
- stating her concerns…but so gently the severity of the concerns is lost
- avoid and put off stating how much this hurts because you don't want to hurt his feelings
- deciding that the hassle of letting him know that this isn't working for you isn't worth it because you know that he will minimize, joke around, blow you off, or start a fight that won't end until you give in and go quiet, and smile nicely

…and meanwhile, the marriage is rotting silently from the inside out.

It is very unfortunate he doesn't notice on his own. It is also very unfortunate that you protect him from the knowing his marriage is heading towards its demise. He's taught you that he won't hear and won't respond, and so it's just easier not to try. He can find the wiggle room to fool himself that it is "just your time of the month", or the baby has kept you up, or…

I've met men like your husbands, and they will be completely bamboozled when you leave. Because they are clueless about how difficult it is for you.

***

Can I ask you a favor, wife-who-is-lonely?

Can you find a way to make it crystal clear that this isn't working and that he needs to step up?

Do it in a way he **can't** miss it. Let him know that you aren't just complaining about the glass on the counter, or about one night with the guys, or about how he didn't empty the dishwasher yesterday.

Let him know this is a serious situation where you long to be known and understood by the man who once had you feel like you were the most important person in the world. Tell him that there is deep concern about the long term fundamental wellbeing of this marriage. Share that he is missing out on meaningful engagement with you as his wife.

This isn't whining. You aren't griping. You are looking him in the eye and respecting him enough to raise an important issue before it is too late.

Make it different from all the other conversations you've ever had about this. Find a way to have him feel the gravity of it. Maybe you'll have to do something drastic in a creative, significant, even very serious way that creates a shift that he can't ignore. Let him know that you're tired and missing him, and longing for him to be in tune with you…and the consequences of not doing some relationship repair will be dire. That at some point, you may leave the marriage formally because for you, the marriage will actually have been dead for some time.

This won't be mean or bitchy.

To let him know that this marriage is not working for you is the ultimate act of kindness from you to him.

Because he needs to know that if this marriage isn't working for one of you, it isn't working for either of you.

Even if it feels to him like the marriage is good for him as is, if it isn't sustainable and he gets left alone, that will suck for him. Big time.

Can I ask you another favor?

When you let him know, with absolute clarity and huge vulnerability and great courage, would you also give him the benefit of the doubt? Don't label him a jerk. Don't call him names. Be respectful and remind him of how he matters enough to you to risk being open with him. Remind him of your vows, your dreams and hopes together. Challenge him to align his behavior with his core values of love for family and for you. It's quite possible that he really loves you, and he is not aware of how much he takes you for granted.

His behavior is not good, but if you attack his character rather than his behavior, he doesn't have a lot of room to respond positively. You want him to leave the conversation knowing that you believe he can do better, because he is better than that.

***

He might be really pissed.

I mean, really, *really* pissed.

No guy likes to know that the person who matters most to him finds him falling short. It is so much easier to be pissed than crushed, devastated, or deeply regretful, especially for men. Give him a day or two to wrap his head around it. Let him calm down, and then talk about it.

But you should know that a lot of men are going to hope that situation will "blow over" in a few days.

Don't let it blow over.

Calmly and assertively let him know that no action is experienced as continued disengagement, and you are really pulling for him to invest in the relationship. Many will find counseling a great option. A therapist can help your husband understand his behaviour. Therapists don't believe in blaming people; counselors stand for changing patterns to be constructive.

Some of you might do a marriage enrichment weekend, engage in an online course. Take a survey. There's lots of great resources to be found online.

Others of you might just benefit from reading books, Friends of mine each purchased the same popular book about vital marriages, and have formed a mini-book club. Just the two of them. They highlight the parts that seem relevant, and compare what each wrote. They write in the margins about how what they are reading applies to them. And then they sit down with each other to go through the book, page by page, reading it out loud to each other, and stopping as often as they need to, to really figure out how to relate it to their own marriage.

He won't go to therapy? Watch movies! There is research that says that couples that watch a movie together from a designated list of movies and then discuss them afterwards can have substantial improvements in their relationships.[iv] (Remember though, the value of this occurs with good discussion after the movie.)

Do *something*.

And then try something else if it doesn't work for both of you.

Change the trajectory of your marriage. Don't let him silently coerce you to remain in a marriage that you know is slowly dying. Be clear with him that continuing with his benign disengagement actually is destructive, and make it hard for him to fool himself otherwise.

Here's to hoping you find the strength to pull off what is truly the most challenging and important conversation of your life!

3 BEFORE IT IS TOO LATE…

I was talking recently to some of my colleagues about couple therapy.

One of the topics that came up was the reluctance of one partner to hear the other spouse's pain—and do something about it.

Sometimes, when couples come to therapy, it is very apparent one has very much wanted to come, and the other is coming very reluctantly. It's then a therapist asks the couples which one is the "draggee" in therapy, and one the "dragger".

A therapist mentioned the painful scenario of having a couple come into therapy after one spouse has said:

Enough. I'm done:

- Enough of the distance.
- Enough of trying to make the partner hear of the loneliness.
- Enough of pleading, trying to make something happen.
- Enough of saying, "We need to talk to somebody. We need to figure this out."

- Enough of trying to have their spouse hear that this isn't just some disgruntlement about the schedule or the chores. This isn't some bickering or complaining that will pass.
- Enough of not being heard.
- Enough of not being seen and valued

The exhausted, burned out spouse says:

"Enough. I'm not doing this anymore. I'm done."

And means it.

***

Suddenly the spouse hears has heard the pain, and understands the seriousness of the marital crisis. The one who has been trying for so long, has started packing. The years of effort are over.

The spouse now "gets it"--*big time.*

The spouse kicks into high gear (because all along he really did want to be married, but complacency has solidly set in), and in horror and shock, begins to plead for the marriage.

***

Sincerely, dedicatedly, and earnestly, the spouse:

- Books the counseling appointment
- Tries to start conversations, writes long letters of love and commitment, texts love and commitment multiple times per day
- Now comes home from work on time
- Fixes the things that have been on the "to do list" for months
- Actively participates in childcare
- Shows up at the kids' games

...doing all the things that have been complained about for years.

The imminence of divorce propels action in frenetic ways.

Only it's too late.

When "enough" was said, it was *too late*.

The last chances had already been offered and re-offered, and had already been pulled off the table.

When one therapist said this to the rest of us, there were sad smiles of knowing all around the room. We've all seen these couples and its painful.

The sad part is when these couples show up for therapy, the draggee has become the dragger, and now, the dragger has become the draggee.

The spouse that has been begging and pleading for years is done with the marriage. They come to therapy only to have the therapist's help to explain that there is no more opportunity to work on this. We generally only see these couples once, because there is nothing to do, nothing to work on. There is no will on the part of the one who is done to re-engage. She will say she's tried over and over for years, and is **done trying.**

The spouse that hadn't been accessible and responsive really is sincere about wanting to make the marriage work (and has wanted to be married all along). And as motivated as they now might be, there is no space to make the marriage work—because **there is no marriage** anymore.

The marriage disintegrated in front of their eyes, but they didn't see it: their eyes were glued to the video game, the football game, the beer in front of them, or the project at work.

Statistically, frankly, this spouse is most often (though not nearly always) male.

The long pattern of distancing isn't about being a jerk. This distancing is about *the challenge of being intimate with someone in a culture that ridicules vulnerability and makes it difficult.* It's about pulling away from someone who makes him feel like he is never enough and can never measure up.

It's turning away from something he feels lousy at, to move towards an area where he has the sense of competence--like his job or the basketball team, or an area of mindless numbing--like video games or alcohol.

So often, a man values and loves his wife, and wants a good marriage, but doesn't know how, and he pulls away from the uncomfortable feelings...

...and doesn't realize that this results in pulling away from his life's love in ways that seem intolerable to you.

***

This book is designed to start an important conversation.

This book is for her...to develop language and courage to speak up; to have difficult conversations that seem easier to not have on any given day—except then they might never occur. This book is for you to contemplate if the high price of making change is actually lower than the high price of staying silent in a relationship where the drift creates an ever widening distance.

This book is for him...show him sections that stand out to you. Highlight bits you want him to see. This book can be a powerful symbol to him that change is required...a slowing of schedules, an increased engagement, a step up to participate more in the tasks of the household. This book is to help him hear how desperate you are to connect with him in a meaningful way.

This book dares you to figure out how to make this work for both of you...before it's too late.

4 *TOO MUCH* CAN SQUASH A MARRIAGE

Boiling water for tea is a good thing, except when it's *too much*.

And when it's too much, it's just not a good thing. Even though boiling water for tea is a fairly benign activity.

Let me explain.

At our office, we don't use the harsh overhead fluorescent lights in the counseling rooms. My thinking is that uncovering and exposing parts of oneself is hard enough without feeling like you are under glaring floodlights. So the overhead lights are off, and there is much more muted and soft lighting from several floor and desk lamps in each of the counseling offices.

In the cooler months, our offices feel the chill. Being a corner office, we have two outside walls, and the heating from the main furnace doesn't warm it up enough. So we have space heaters in each office and the main area. People are feeling "on edge" often when they come to see us; warming up the environment and increasing the *cozy factor* is important. (Which all sounds so altruistic. To be frank, it's hard for me to facilitate good therapy with a client when my teeth are chattering and my fingers are cold. It works for me, too.)

Melanie, our office manager, likes to work under the fluorescents, so they are on in the main office area where she is. However, she also has a desk lamp on her desk. Our fabulous interior designer, Robyn, says that a person is 30 percent more productive with a desk lamp. I'm all over research...thus the lamp. The "30 percent productivity increase" has become something of office lore.

Our administration space is, ahem, very efficient in its use of space (which is another way of saying a terribly cramped). So our "kitchen" is contained in a piece of furniture that was originally built as an armoire. We use the lower drawers for office supplies, and what would normally hold a television now is the "kitchen"--it holds a little fridge, our microwave and kettle.

With the lamps on in the counseling room, and on Melanie's desk, the fridge going, and then, starting in the fall, the space heaters—when we plug in the kettle to make tea—all at once, it goes dark and silent.

The breaker pops because we are drawing too much power on a circuit.

And Melanie makes a dash to the breaker panel to bring the lights back on in the therapy session next door.

By Christmas, Melanie will have retrained us...before we put the kettle on, we unplug the heater and announce to her that we will be decreasing her efficiency (temporarily) by 30 percent.

The kettle itself is not the problem. The heaters' seasonal use is not the problem. The lamps aren't the problem.

The problem is having too many of them drawing power all at once from a system that has finite levels of capability...and exceeding that capacity.

***

Exhaustion has become something of a status symbol in our culture. When people say, "How are you?", one of the common (and unfortunately, respected) answers is "Really busy" or "Really tired" or "Very stressed".

How is it that we, as a culture, esteem those who are maxed out?

Somewhere along the line, people determine their value on their level of productivity. With our very value on the line, folks exhaust themselves to prove how valuable they are, maybe even indispensable.

When a person's value is based on their productivity, exhaustion is the logical, even inevitable, outcome. When a parent's worth as a parent hinges on how many activities that their children are involved in, and being there to watch every game, and sit through every lesson, the children and parents are overbooked and overloaded.

There is a cost to relationships when either or both partners are exhausted. Some circuit breakers somewhere in the relationship break at some point, because *too much is: Just. Too. Much.*

***

I had a conversation with a colleague recently who wryly commented that breaking her arm had been the best thing that could have happened to her marriage this summer.

She couldn't golf with her buddies, nobody asked her to play as a sub for the baseball team, she couldn't take on new projects in the yard, and so on. Because of her injury, by necessity, she had to just *be*.

She was less exhausted because she didn't/couldn't have as much on her "to do" list. With the extra time and the extra "gas in her tank", she and her husband had a renaissance of sorts in their relationship. They spent time walking in the neighborhood, got hooked on a series on Netflix that they would watch together (and dissect after). They cooked together and ate together more than they had in years.

And she loved it.

***

Years ago, my insurance agent encouraged me to purchase "catastrophic illness insurance" so that if I contracted any number of serious medical illnesses, I would be immediately entitled to a large cash payment. While it could be used towards unexpected medical expenses, he said that many people had life changing mind-set changes, where they might want to take a trip with their families, or cut back on how hard they were working. He noted that in the face of catastrophic illness, there was often a shift in priorities towards relationships and creating memories. This insurance could accommodate for these shifts by allowing a person to pull back from their financial obligations.

I was horrified, and still am, at this thought.

One of my most heartfelt prayers for my life is that I would not need a "wake up call" like a catastrophic illness to be fully alive to the relationships that are important to me. I don't want a diagnosis to prompt me to adjust my schedule to something that works.

I want to make choices to live out what I know to be important now, while I'm healthy.

***

The little important things—the touch of romance with lighting a candle for the meal, cutting a blossom and bringing it inside to put in a vase, rubbing sore feet at the end of the day, or drawing a hot bath for a spouse—these small acts of love are important, but can so easily get lost in the midst of the busy-ness. Those miniature expressions of kindness and care take time and energy, which often does not exist in our maxed-out culture.

Checking Facebook (and YouTube, and Twitter, and email and a blog and the news highlights and...), taking on another project at work, accepting the promotion, figuring out how to move to a bigger house, enrolling the kids in one more sport, agreeing to one more committee—all of these can put us into situations where we max out the circuit and somethings gotta give.

None of these are bad, but the stress on the system is HUGE.

For some couples I have seen for couple counseling, the therapy session serves as the only time in the week where they are able to be 100 percent focused on each other. Where a couple has a chance to listen deeply, and the only opportunity to feel heard (and valued and appreciated) by their partner. The rest of the week is too much of a scramble. There is no other time possible to simply sit quietly with each other, and focus on themselves as a couple.

I think sometimes folks put investing in their marriage "on hold" when things get busy, and promise themselves that they will tend to it, when they can, later. If later ever comes. When the circuit is too full, even full of good stuff, the breaker can turn it all off.

It's heartbreaking to watch a couple come in with their marriage in serious crisis simply because there have been far too many draws of energy.

A marriage cannot survive unlimited additions of tasks, interests, distractions and stressors--even good things. Any relationship will collapse under the onslaught of prolonged overscheduling.

The breaker will pop.

How much power are you drawing off? Let me tell you that I have personally witnessed folks who have spent years driving their children around to many lessons and practices, had grueling work schedules to generate enough income for a certain standard of living. They drive themselves to exhaustion. Folks run themselves into the ground, "for the sake of the family".

Your family wants your husband even more than they want his raise. You want your husband's time and energy and investment more than you want a new car or an expensive vacation, right? Your family doesn't benefit when you are exhausted from extra efforts to make a wonderful home. Your children may complain if they can't get the newest gaming system, but that pain pales in comparison to not having two parents engaged with them, playing in the yard or cheering from the bleachers.

You might want to consider calling your husband over to read this. It might be that the two of you have distance between you because one or both of you have such full plates that your marriage isn't being nurtured.

A neglected relationship deteriorates.

Have a discussion about how to recalibrate your energies, and decide what to choose to take out of your life before life makes decisions for you.

Know that too much of a good thing is too much. You could lose the **important** as you get distracted by the **urgent**.

5 DISENGAGEMENT...THE SILENT, SLIPPERY BETRAYAL

Have you even thought of disengagement as betrayal?

We usually think of betrayal in terms of infidelity—affairs. For example, when a partner is unfaithful in engaging in a sexual relationship with another. Or when a partner has an intimate emotional relationship even if it doesn't culminate with sex in the relationship.

Other common betrayals which hit the must-go-see-therapist-in-crisis threshold?

- significant financial mismanagement or secret spending resulting in the discovery of a scary pile of debt
- drug use or obsessive porn viewing or gambling discovery. The disclosure of a secret, the discovery of engagement in an undesirable activity, and often a hefty red number on the line of credit, or the discovery of a hidden credit card statement

It is absolutely necessary to deal with the shock and horror that has a couple reeling after a cataclysmic betrayal. Looking the other way and continuing on like it didn't happen is rather like building on sand. It might look good on the outside, but inside of each partner is insecurity, fear, sadness and mistrust. Underneath what looks fine actually lies a shaky foundation.

A good deal of the time, however, a silent, more insidious betrayal is discovered...a betrayal begun a long time before one of those obvious betrayals, slowly eroding the foundation of the relationship, priming it for disaster: Disengagement.

Brene Brown writes about disengagement in her best-selling book, *Daring Greatly*:

> In fact, this betrayal usually happens long before the other ones. I'm talking about the betrayal of disengagement. Of not caring. Of letting the connection go. Of not being willing to devote time and effort to the relationship. The word betrayal evokes experiences of cheating, lying, breaking a confidence, failing to defend us to someone else who's gossiping about us, and not choosing us over other people. These behaviors are certainly betrayals, but they're not the only form of betrayal. If I had to choose the form of betrayal that emerged most frequently from my research and that was the most dangerous in terms of corroding the trust connection, I would would say disengagement.[v]

Let me be clear, people...this ain't no frivolous line I found in some obscure book.

This is something that we see regularly at our counseling office. Often when couples show up with a marriage in shambles, disengagement has had an enormous, though largely hidden, effect on the marriage.

Disengagement is sneaky.

Disengagement is hard to name. So it's hard to talk about. And harder to actually figure out what to do about it.

The betrayal of disengagement is:

- Often written off as a partner "making a mountain out of a molehill".
- Pawned off as "well, boys will be boys", giving a legitimacy to the practice of ignoring the primary relationship in a husband's life. He spends night after night watching hockey with the guys, a beer in his hand.
- Explained/rationalized as necessary e.g. "I have to put all these hours in at the business or it will fail." How do you argue against a line like that?
- Minimized as insignificant: "C'mon, it's only hanging out in the workshop getting little things done…it's my alone time. It's not like I'm having an affair with a woman. What's the big deal? Don't you want me to enjoy my life?"

When a partner feels disengagement, and raises the concern:

- She is called out as being whiny or a drama queen.
- She dares not express the loneliness because you know what's coming…She's going to be labelled as a needy or worse yet, *high maintenance*. Why would any woman want to raise the issue of a partner's disengagement if that will happen?
- She simply doesn't have the opportunity to raise the concern because some level of engagement would be required to even start the conversation...and between the incredible number of hours at work, and the children: They. Never. Connect.

Brené Brown also says:

> When the people we love or with whom we have a deep connection stop caring, stop paying attention, stop investing and fighting for the relationship, trust begins to

slip away and hurt starts seeping in. Disengagement triggers shame and our greatest fears - the fears of being abandoned, unworthy, and unlovable. What can make this covert betrayal so much more dangerous than something like a lie or an affair is that we can't point to the source of our pain - there's no event, no obvious evidence of brokenness. It can feel crazy-making.[vi]

"There's no event, no obvious evidence of brokenness. It can feel crazy making." Does that feel like truth inside of you when you read it?

***

The cost of disengagement is high—**very** high. It takes a toll on the relationship. It creates a vulnerability in the relationship as broad as a barn door for the marriage to become like the walking dead. It looks like it's all there, but so not.

The cost of disengagement is a hollow marriage, that limps along with a focus on the children, with little more in common than a mailing address. Both partners are disengaged, and don't invest in the relationship to change it.

Sometimes, in desperation, the partner that has experienced the disengagement resorts to behaviour that is out of line with his/her values to cope with the pain of the fears and shame. An affair. Alcohol. Excessive shopping. We all know what happens in these situations.

And it ain't pretty. Trust me.

I don't know of anyone who has entered a marriage thinking,

- "When it gets hard or busy or risky, I'm going to pull away without acknowledging it."
- "When I am not heard, I'll give up trying"
- "If my spouse doesn't hear me when I express a concern, I'll just pull away and put my interests elsewhere."

Nobody does that.

Not intentionally, anyway.

***

Inviting a partner to authentic engagement is risky, daring, courageous work.

It means raising a stink over something that is covert, hidden and insidious. Your partner probably won't understand. Your partner may be frustrated with you seemingly making something out of nothing. A partner who is disengaged often doesn't do it intentionally or maliciously. The drift happened without conscious notice.

It's hard to raise an issue when it feels like your concern could be brushed off. That often feels like you've been brushed off…and nobody likes that.

***

You may want to show your partner this chapter…to show your partner that you are not crazy, you are not making this up, that the distance between the two of you has a name: *disengagement*. And your partner can learn that with disengagement, there is pain. Always. For both.

It might mean calling in a therapist to help you say to your partner, "I am intolerably lonely. And this situation is not sustainable," with the therapist helping you be heard. The experience of disengagement then becomes a conversation with a therapist, and that gives you the space to work at it differently. You can figure out how to work at it.

Re-engaging may prevent some rash, inappropriate and highly expensive behaviour that will create social, relational, family, psychological costs for years to come. Extramarital affairs are sometimes a logical outcome of disengagement. I'm not legitimizing infidelity as an inevitable result. I'm describing reality.

Take some time to think about the level of engagement you each have in the relationship? When did it change? How did it change? What are the acts of engagement that you used to do that you've dropped? What would it take for you to re-engage with those behaviors? What do you miss that your spouse used to do? Can you talk about it? If it's hard to talk about it, can you have a conversation about how hard it is to talk about it?

**And husband of the person reading this book? If your partner has called you over to look at this page, please know that it is serious. Engage in a curious, compassionate conversation that explores why she wanted you to read it. Please? Know that being shown this chapter is a tentative, brave and maybe desperate signal to wake up and pay attention. Being shown this chapter, quite simply, is a gift that I'm inviting you to accept. A hard gift (painful, but given out of care and desire to make things better)

6 WORK ON THE CONNECTION, NOT THE COMMUNICATION

"We all fear facing life alone and we all long for loving connection – a hand to hold that changes our world to a safer place and soothes our brain."[vii]

Dr. Susan Johnson

EFT guru

Often, when couples come for help on their relationship, and our client care manager, Melanie, asks them on the phone why they are coming, the response will be: they can't communicate. The couple wants to work on their communication.

It's funny that couples ask for help with "communication". Often, these are professionals that are highly capable and competent communicators in their role of physicians, lawyers, executives, line foreman, human resource manager, or executive assistant. Bakers, mechanics, accountants...all have to communicate to help their job go smoothly.

Highly capable individuals with an incredible ability to express themselves come to marital therapy asking for help in communication. And they are right—when they attempt to speak to their spouse, they get defensive and non-productive. They watch themselves be hostile and self-protective, instead of collaborative. Spouses snap at their partner in ways they wouldn't dream of doing at work. When they try to explain themselves, their ability to be articulate disappears and they stumble over their words. They can't even think to come up with helpful responses, and instead watch nasty barbs explode out of their mouths towards their spouse in ways that they would be embarrassed if friends or colleagues were there to witness it.

There is an occasional couple that requires some skill training to know what it looks like to speak respectfully, how to inquire further about another person's opinion, and how to navigate a conflict. There are some that have never been around kind and gentle discussion that opens the door to productive dialogue. Very occasionally, education and skill practice is helpful.

However, what is much more often the case is that the connection between the couple is the issue. Once the connection is repaired, the communication ceases to become an issue. It's hard to communicate to communicate deeply and effectively with your spouse when you aren't sure the spouse has got your back.

***

I'm a science geek...I love to learn things. To know what works, and how it works, and what we can learn from understanding our world better using scientific research.

We were created for relationships. We need relationships to survive. Relationships are as important to our health as oxygen, food, water and sunshine. Without relationships we suffer.

Loneliness is just as much of a risk to our health as moderate smoking or obesity.[viii] We need relationships.

Simply: we require connection.

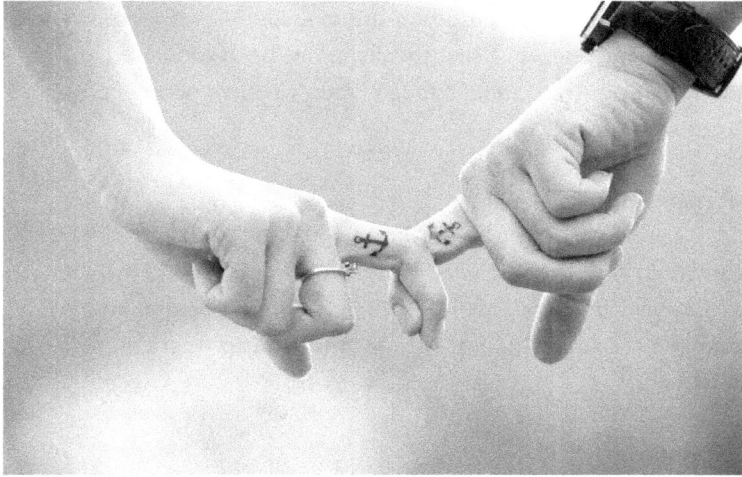

The anchors on those fingers? Yeah…being loved does that.

Feeling secure, knowing you belong--it anchors a person. And when a person is securely anchored, it creates a sense of balance. Rather like when I learned to play basketball…feet shoulder width apart, knees slightly bent, weight over both feet, arms held up in front--this was known as the "triple threat position"…this balanced and anchored position put a person in optimal position to pass, shoot or dribble.

Being loved in a meaningful relationship does that in our lives…we are better able to tackle challenges, have difficult conversations, and move forward effectively.

Our brains do better, we function better, we can solve problems better, and we move through the world more effectively when we have meaningful, life giving relationships in our lives. There are all sorts of scientific results that demonstrate that to us objectively and clearly.

We know that couples do better when they are connected. We all do better when we have meaningful connections with family and a few significant friends. Scientifically, it has been measured and shown that our lives are enhanced when we have people in our corner that are A.R.E.:

Accessibility:

I can reach you. When I need you, I can find you. You are there for me. Physical and emotional availability. When I need help, or reassurance, or simply want some contact, I can trust you that you are there.

Responsive:

I can rely on you to hear me and respond When I say something, you respond. You let me know that I matter. Your voice, your body language, your timing tells me that you hear me and you are important to me.

Engaged:

You connect with me...meaningfully. I can tell that you're in the conversation, that the relationship is something that you're working at. You decrease my isolation and increase connection. This is one step beyond available and responsive...you may be around to see me upset about my day, but if you tell me that I'm silly and over reacting, you aren't engaged with my distress...I will feel disconnected from you.[ix]

Being available, responsive and engaged changes how we respond

34

to our world. Husbands and wives that ARE there for each other is a combination that is incredible.

A couple becomes more resilient, tolerant, creative, relaxed, energized, confident and capable when they ARE present for their spouse.

The question husbands and wives need to ask is not: "Can we communicate?" but rather, "Are we connected?" Connected people can use the communication ability that they had early on in the relationship, and still have with friends and colleagues.

A.R.E. you connected as a couple?

7 THE HIDDEN DANGERS OF OVERFUNCTIONING

I hurt my back several months ago. The physiotherapist said I likely ruptured a disc in my lower back. The resulting pain has been more in my leg than in my back. The sciatic pain has been quite high for several months.

I went to see Mike. Mike is a professor of physiotherapy at the University. I met him when I taught there, and I like his work. As a systems therapist, I value when people work to notice a problem and then don't just work to fix the problem, but track back to see where the problem arose...and then explore how it was that problem came about. When I've taken Junior Tribe Members to see him, he has effectively fixed back problems by addressing the ankle, or knee problems by addressing issues in the trunk.

As Mike is assessing my back a few weeks ago, he does a simple test. He has me lie on my tummy and lift one leg at a time off the plinth a few inches from my hip. I can do it on each side--on my left and my right leg. It's a lot of work on my left side, and not as comfortable, but I can do it.

And he says: "Ahhhh!", like he just learned something exceedingly important.

Follow me carefully here: He has me put my hand on my gluteal muscles (affectionately called "gluts" by those in the biz...the big chunky muscles in the butt) and says: "Feel your right butt cheek when you lift your leg up".

I put my hand on my butt cheek...and my right glut tightens to lift my leg.

He says, "Now, feel your left butt cheek when you lift your left leg up."

My leg goes up...but my left gluts stay soft. It stays squishy. (Sorry—too much information from a therapist?) It was weird to feel the marked difference in the way the muscle groups were acting.

And he goes on to explain..."Two muscle groups—the hamstrings [the muscles in the back of your leg] and the gluteal muscles should be sharing together in the work of extending your leg up. The system is wonky on your left side. Your hamstrings are doing *all* the work, and your left gluts aren't firing."

***

Mike then goes on to tell me what marriage counseling had long ago deeply ingrained in me:

When one part underfunctions, the whole thing can still work if *another part over functions.*

He then went on to tell me the implications of the pairing of an over functioning muscle group with an under functioning muscle group for my body.

Mike didn't actually need to tell me.

I could have given him the lecture...because I've seen marriages die with this pattern never being addressed.

When one part underfunctions and another part over functions to compensate, it pulls the relationship out of alignment. And being out of alignment creates all sorts of related issues.

It works...but *at a price*. Pain. Decreased strength. Fatigue.

***

My recent back injury taught me about the pain and discomfort when one set of muscles under function and another set of muscles compensate to overfunction.

Underfunctioners often don't realize that they are underfunctioning...they just aren't awake in their life. They don't realize others are looking after the practical and emotional demands in the world around them. They may also not realize the long term cost of allowing a partner in life/work/friendship to do most/all of the work. Underfunctioning is a relationship killer.

But...drum roll please...Overfunctioning is also a relationship killer.

***

Most of us grow up thinking being kind is a good thing.

And it is.

But kindness that robs others of their ability to fulfill their roles in the world that is not *kind*.

That's *enablement*.

***

Overfunctioning is treating someone as if they can't do it for themselves.

It's saying, "I don't trust you to fold your laundry, so I'll do it".

Overfunctioning is disrespectful.

It's saying, "I can't see your abilities or trust them. Move over and I'll do it. "

Overfunctioning is dismissive.

It's saying, "I don't believe you are capable of paying for this yourself, so of course I'll buy it for you," or "I will agree with you that you don't need to participate. I won't make us both uncomfortable by insisting that I need you to show up in our lives. The kids and I can live our lives without you."

In essence, "You're not that important or capable...I can do without you."

Overfunctioning is disempowering.

It's taking away *that feeling* from someone. You know, that feeling--that rush that happens when you work hard and git'er done. That feeling of doing your job right. That feeling of, "I don't feel like it, but I'll have that important but awkward conversation with our teenager, because I can contribute". That feeling of, "It was hard. Really hard. And I got it done!" Gosh, that feeling is good! That "I can put my head down on my pillow peacefully tonight for a job well done today" feeling. That, "Whew, that was brave and hard and scary, but I DID IT!!" feeling.

Overfunctioners rob underfunctioners.

They teach their loved ones--the underfunctioners, that they are incapable, not-good-enough, and simply not competent.

Oh, overfunctioners don't say these things in words, at all. They don't even think it in their heads. Matter of fact, most overfunctioners will be horrified to read this...and may not recognize it.

But trust me, overfunctioners will read this. The whole thing. It's in their nature. They can't help it!

***

A friend of mine, a lovely woman, came by her over functioning honestly. I love her. It was a natural result from her survival strategies, which were actually adaptive for her in her life. She was a perfectionist--and that was a way to survive growing up in a home that had an alcoholic parent.

So, she did all the laundry folding while he watched the game...he didn't mind being able to focus on the game. And she loved that all the corners were lined up on the towels. She fed the dog, because then she knew the dog wasn't being overfed. She bought the groceries, and put them away in exacting order, and cleaned the bathroom, just so. Everything...all the rest of the house, just perfect. I could go on. If she did it, then she knew it was done right. She liked the feeling of doing it herself so she could ensure it all met her standards.

And then, over the years, she became a ball of resentment, because she was exhausted...and her husband was still watching the game.

He was happy...until he saw that she wasn't happy. He was a great guy, really. Just blithely clueless until the day she said, "Enough".

He agreed to go to therapy.

When they went to therapy, she learned to turn to her husband over the course of the week, and in a very deliberate (and humorous, really) manner, she turns directly to face him, and would say, "I AM DROPPING THE BALL!" and with her hands, she would mimic the action of dropping the ball.

That was the hint that he needed to pick up the ball and look around. Fold the laundry. Make supper. Clean up the kitchen.

He actually needed some coaching to wake up and notice, at first. She rather trained the *looking around* right out of him.

This wasn't just about getting him do more chores. Nope, actually, by that time, chores were the least of their worries.

See, the problems were more than about tasks like emptying the dishwasher. She was overfunctioning in *every area* of their relationship.

She was making sure that their lives worked in just about every way. She knew what his favorite restaurants were and made reservations at those places. She spent less so he could spend more. She placated him in arguments, and generally invested more in their lives than he was.

And that wasn't healthy for anybody.

As they continued therapy, and she functioned less, he could pick up some slack.

This whole process wasn't without its moments--scary, anxious moments.

She wondered what would happen if she chose to go out and leave him to make supper.

The therapist said he would make supper. Like a capable adult.

Or he wouldn't.

He needed to understand what happened when he didn't make supper. It would be uncomfortable for him...and she would likely be irked, a normal response to someone goofing up. And they would deal with it.

Natural outcomes.

He needed to be trusted to function. He wasn't incapable.

He needed:

- to be given permission to fail,
- time to figure out what needed to get done
- to do it his way, and
- the space to actively participate in the relationship.

***

Picture this: 2 people standing in a canoe.

Pretty tippy image, isn't it?

Both need to be attuned to the actions of others to keep the canoe balanced. If one leans out one way, even a little, the other needs to lean the other way to keep it balanced.

If one leans out a lot, the other leans out a lot the other way...and the canoe stays stable.

The canoe won't tip if the two are leaning way out in different directions, as long as they balance each other out.

The canoe is stable...and it's not tipping. And the two in the canoe stay dry—they aren't in the water.

But they sure aren't comfortable.

And it probably isn't sustainable.

And ultimately, the canoe is at greater risk of capsizing. It's exhausting to ensure the boat doesn't tip by leaning so far out to match the other...

It's. Just. Plain. Hard.

The underfunctioning/overfunctioning dynamic is a partnership just like that.

We can over function with children, with co-workers and friends—and husbands.

Overfunctioners work super hard...and generally with the best intentions--*consciously*. They do what they do at personal cost to benefit the greater good.

The advantages to overfunctioning aren't always conscious.

Overfunctioners get advantages that are beyond their conscious awareness. Overfunctioners get to:

- feel like a hero...like they are rescuing folks who need them desperately. If they keep someone in their lives at less than full capacity, they get feel good about themselves. Who doesn't like to be a rescuer?
- control their world. How many of us haven't done all the work of the group project at school because then we knew we would get the A?

Overfunctioning:

- is the ultimate in quality control.
- is the ultimate in avoiding conflict. If you just do everything, there's no need to argue about it, with anybody.
- is a very safe way to keep the peace. No challenging required.
- ensures you are needed. If you train people to need you, then they can't leave you. It might even make it hard for them to be mad at you. Being needed means you are pseudo-secure in the relationship.

As much as overfunctioners resent the role and complain about it...they can refuse to give it up.

Equalizing the relationship means brave conversations and courageous self-awareness. It means holding space for uncertainty and discomfort as the old painful but familiar ruts are left for establishing new ways of being together.

8 THE HIDDEN COST OF UNDERFUNCTIONING

It stands to reason that with every overfunctioner, there is an underfunctioner.

As I mentioned in the last chapter, Mike, my physiotherapist, found that one set of muscles was not firing as he was working on my back. He wanted to work with me to solve the dysfunctional muscle pattern of one muscle group doing the work of two muscle groups, while the second one took a holiday.

My body was out of alignment. It was making my back and leg pain worse. There were all sorts of related issues.

The over/underfunctioning works—but *at a huge price*. Pain. Decreased strength. Fatigue.

***

The solution, as Mike told me, was as simple as it was profound:

The strategy to fix the underfunctioning/ overfunctioning dysfunction is **to get the under functioning muscles to start firing.**

So, Mike taught me to work to first tighten my left butt cheek and then lift my left leg. I had to reteach the muscles that weren't working how to get involved again.

The way to fixing this was to teach those underfunctioning muscles to do their share, with awareness and repetition and practice and strengthening.

It was weird...I had to "find" the muscle and figure out what signals to send to it to get it to contract.

It wasn't that the gluteal muscles didn't want to work...it was more like it had forgotten how.

It wasn't easy at first.

But even after two sets of 10 in the office on that visit, those glut muscles were already just starting to begin to do what it was supposed to do.

I do this exercise every night now before I go to bed. My left gluts still only work about 80-90 percent of what the right side can do.

But this, combined with the other exercises Mike has given me, meant marked improvement. In the last week or so, I have begun to sleep through the night without pain medication for the first time in months.

Fixing this under/overfunctioning pattern in my gluts and hamstrings has literally changed my daily life.

***

Underfunctioners often don't realize that they are underfunctioning. They just aren't awake in their life. Underfunctioners don't realize others are looking after the practical and emotional demands in the world around them. They may also not realize the long term cost of allowing a partner in life/work/friendship to do most/all of the work.

They may not understand how their underfunctioning is a relationship killer.

***

My husband, Jim, has told me a story of how, early in their marriage, his late wife, Car, ran an experiment, leaving a load of folded laundry on the stairs to see how long it might take until he saw it and carried it upstairs to put away.

After several days she gave up.

She let him know what it was like for her to do the laundry and not have him notice or think to pitch in.

Jim never forgot. He realized how he had unwittingly gone around that laundry basket several times a day. It was like he didn't see it, even as he repeatedly did a little two step to avoid it.

After she talked to him about the laundry basket, and the resentment she was developing because of his persistent ignorance of it, he started to see it.

Jim is a thoughtful laundry do-er now.

I'm grateful that Jim was married to someone before he met me that taught him some important life lessons that made him more compassionate and understanding. He tells me that his first wife taught him how to be a better husband.

***

Underfunctioner—take note:

You've likely never heard of underfunctioning. You likely wouldn't trouble yourself to look it up.

Chances are you are reading this because your spouse says it's super important for you to read.

If so, consider it a gift?

It might seem easier to let your spouse regularly do the cleanup. It might be a convenient excuse to say you suck at folding laundry. You might beg off grocery shopping or driving the kids because you're tired and you've worked hard.

Underfunctioning is far more than just about chores. It's also about investment into the maintenance and upkeep of the relationship. It's easier and less vulnerable to not start hard conversations or invest in sharing your heart, so you might just choose to not start a conversation—turning the television on is easier. Not checking in on her, not finding out what is or isn't working for her is one more way you may not be holding up your end of the relationship.

There are some significant short term perks to being an underfunctioner.

And your spouse may well pick up the slack, even with an attempt to be understanding.

It might help to know that overfunctioners are willing to over function quite a long time...because:

- it's easier to do it than explain and invite you to participate. It's an uncomfortable conversation to tell someone that they aren't stepping up.
- they come from a world where one parent overfunctioned while the other underfunctioned and it's all they know.
- they have spent time explaining and cajoling and arguing and you have blown them off. They have simply given up on you.

However, marriages where one spouse is consistently underfunctioning while the other one overfunctions are at serious risk. It creates an atmosphere of resentment and distance. It sets the tone where disengagement is very possible.

The sad thing with the dynamic of an overfunctioning/underfunctioning marriage is that it limps along, with everything getting done and everything mostly looking ok—until one day, the overfunctioner can't do it anymore.

The marriage has been silently eroding for a very long time and can seem to collapse overnight.

Marriages work best when the two work together to find a rhythm that works for both—when they work in tandem.

Underfunctioner, if your significant other has troubled you to see this chapter, would you be willing to recognize yourself in it? Would you be willing to recognize that your partner is struggling under the weight of overfunctioning now? And trust me, you as an underfunctioner could pay the ultimate price of losing someone you really care about—if not in body, then in spirit. Being able to watch the game while she runs around getting things done might seem like a good deal. But trust me, you both will pay the price.

If your significant other has had you read this chapter, would you be willing to begin an uncomfortable but ultimately beneficial conversation of curiosity, where you ask lots of questions and reserve your reactions, just to really hear the experience of the overfunctioner in your life?

Would you be willing to notice that you are at serious risk of losing the most important relationship in your life because you benignly choose to omit seeing how much harder your spouse works at your relationship than you?

This isn't just about housework--making supper, laundry, emptying the dishwasher (though it is that too).

This is about:

- Engaging with the kids,
- Starting conversations with your wife about what she is interested in
- Helping with your children's homework
- Pulling out the calendar and being the one to insert the kid's schedules on it
- About raising the conversation of your unresolved last argument to actually pursue its end.
- Taking initiative to write the birthday card to your mother this year (and buying it ahead of time!)
- Arranging the Friday night date this time
- Saying, "I love you" first, not just, "I love you too" in response
- Being the one to pour special glasses of something at the end of the day for you enjoy together

When the underfunctioner, as hard as it can be to get more involved, finds a way to engage, it releases the overfunctioner.

Sometimes you may even need to gently kick the overfunctioner in the butt, as in, "Stop doing all the work and then resenting me for it. I want to share in the work of our lives. Trust me enough to not do it all yourself."

It frees everyone to a marriage that has a good chance of working well.

9 THE IMPERCEPTIBLE, ALMOST IRRESISTABLE SLIDE INTO INFIDELITY

I've worked extensively with couples in the immediate, devastating, agonizing aftermath of the discovery of an affair.

It's hard to watch the couple come in. One partner, whose world has been rocked at its very foundations has puffy eyes, a huge lostness, feeling their world is suddenly very different. There's often a wildness about their eyes, with a frantic wondering: "What else don't I know?"

The other is partner, the unfaithful, is often very contrite, with poor eye contact. Their shoes receive a lot of careful examination. It does something to a person to violate their own moral code in a manner in which they have little understanding. One of the especially hard parts for the cheating partner is to witness the agony of their partner. That is its own special little hell—to watch the one you have committed your life to loving be in complete devastation as the result of your choices. It's not easy to watch someone you love be in such pain knowing you caused it.

For many couples, we take a two pronged approach when they come in to work through infidelity:

1. The *infidelity is a problem* of betrayal that requires healing work
2. The *infidelity is a symptom* of a problem. It exposes a vulnerability between the couple or within one of the partners that created circumstances ripe for an affair to develop. This requires some relationship repair work. Cheating is hard on a marriage, and it's tough coming back from its discovery...but it's possible to develop a marriage that is stronger and more vibrant than before the affair. The affair can be a cue that one or both of you has some work to do in the area of the exposed vulnerability.

There is a style of affair that is difficult for couples to wrap their head around. The one that develops organically, so slowly that it seems impossible to recognize when it started, and then seems impossible to stop once it has begun.

***

Ever heard of the frog in the kettle? It's a poignant image.

If you plop a frog in a pot of piping hot water, it immediately recognizes the discomfort and danger and promptly hops out.

If you put a frog in a pot of cool water and heat it slowly—ever so slowly, the frog never registers the level of danger increasing every so gradually.

The frog allows itself to be cooked.

***

Let's face it: often we spend more waking hours with our colleagues at work than we do with our families. Supportive work environments where colleagues positively encourage each other and collaborate on projects feel good to be in. They inspire creativity, create positivity within people. What's not to love about colleagues also being great friends?

It can be a very slow, very gradual, almost imperceptible slide into hanging out more often, deepening friendship, and a gradual descent into a relationship of intimacy that happens in such a way that one can't even pinpoint when *the line* was crossed.

Affairs often start out with emotional intimacy. They may not ever become sexual, or do so once the affair has already become well established. The damage is substantial even if sexual intimacy never occurs.

And while a relationship can start innocently and slide into infidelity without detection, once a person is in an affair, it's brutally difficult to pull out.

Helen Fisher's, in her TED talk on The Brain in Love, explains the incredibly powerful pull of love:

> People in love have activity in a tiny factory at the base of the brain…Cells that make dopamine…a natural stimulant…part of the brain's reward system…this is below cognitive thinking, below emotions…part of the reptilian core…associated with wanting, with motivation, with focus and craving. *The same area becomes active when you feel the rush of cocaine.*[x]

We know how addictive cocaine is. The motivation/focus/craving for the new hidden/forbidden relationship is biologically incredibly powerful, and virtually irresistible.

The challenge is that this is below conscious thought; out of the realm of rational thinking. Science has shown this powerful passion lasts about 18 months in a relationship—**any** relationship.

A person in an affair can start to think, "I love my spouse, but I'm not *in love* with my spouse" like they love their affair partner.

The short term, cocaine-like passion created in the exciting novelty of a new relationship is tough competition for a stable, secure, loving relationship with routines and patterns.

It's a little like choosing between the Corvette convertible and a 4 door mid-size sedan.

Who wouldn't choose the Corvette for an afternoon? I would!!

As a lifestyle, though, my choice is the sedan—every time. How am I going to cart groceries home, drive the kids, be warm in the frigid cold of winter ? A whole host of other reasons make the mini-van have much more staying power and be my choice.

Besides, this is an imperfect metaphor. The corvette of an affair *inevitably* morphs into a sedan. The corvette from an affair generally doesn't run on all cylinders either. There is no keeping the corvette option.

Relationships start off with the fun of a Corvette convertible—our brains are designed that way. But *relationships are intended to settle* into a comfortable, useful, secure, solid mid-sized vehicle that will provide the richness of a lifetime of a great ride.

***

One of the most fun parts of my job is working with couples about to get married. They don't come in with relationship problems. They come in because they know that premarital counseling is a great idea. Premarital counseling is a great proactive way to create a lifelong partnership.

The couples that come for premarital counseling generally come with a solid and good relationship that they seek to make even better.

It's inspiring to watch these couples invest in their relationship. They hold hands during sessions, speak warmly and supportively of each other, with each other, and to each other.

And they have no idea that there will likely come a day when they will be tempted and have to make a choice about whether to stay faithful. Right now, they can't imagine anything other than total devotion to their partner.

I'm not sure I've ever met a partner at the beginning of a relationship that ever plans to be unfaithful.

But it happens. It is thought somewhere between 30-50 percent of couples will have an episode of cheating where one partner breaks the vows of fidelity. Relationships don't start out with the intention to hurt the other.

It happens. A little tiff has a partner leave in a huff. Then a supportive co-worker asks about the air of upset, and it feels so good to get it one's chest. And later you're embarrassed to tell your partner that you told your supportive co-worker about your fight, and there is a window where a wall should be—and a wall where a window should be.

***

The pre-emptive strike? The way to keep the walls and windows where they should be?

Here it is:

Have a discussion about what appropriate walls and windows[xi] look like in your marriage. A checklist of sorts perhaps.

An ability to monitor and check your behavior against what you've decided is appropriate behavior, what you've decided when you are feeling calm and connected with your spouse, *guidelines you develop together*—and can use when you may not be thinking so clearly.

***

Remember the frog in hot water?

What if the frog (assuming frogs can be this smart—work *with me*) decided to jump out at a set temperature, regardless of how it was feeling? *It would save itself from certain death.*

Similarly, it's helpful to have markers that you've decided as a couple each of you will not cross.

Now comes the hard part: what to do if/when you cross that line. **Because we know it happens.**

It would be sorely tempting to hide that fact; to avoid telling your partner you did something he wouldn't like. The hard part is to "open up the window" to your partner on it. Telling your spouse that you crossed a line with another person is brutally challenging, but it is a votes for the marriage—big time.

How very difficult, but productive, to say something like, "I did something today that I don't think you'll like. And it's something I'm really not proud of. I had lunch with _____ today. Just her and I. I talked about our fight last night. And I regret that. Partly because it she was so supportive and it felt better to talk to her than is healthy. I'm sorry but I wanted to let you know. Now you know more than she does—because you are so important to me, I want you to be the closest one to me."

- That repositions the spouse to be the one "in the know" and most intimate with you.
- That makes it harder for the walls to get thicker in your marriage and windows to get larger in the illicit relationship.
- This is hard, brutally hard. But it opens up a window and lets your partner in. The transparency is admirable.

An equally brutal hard part is for the spouse to hear this and work to not only acknowledge the pain, but **to also realize the value of the window** that is being enlarged and maintained in the relationship. It's hard to appreciate a window when the view through is one that is hurtful. Most often, it will not be heard gratefully. It will be heard with a reaction of hurt. And we know that when people are hurt, they often respond protectively being very angry.

To stay grounded and to be grateful for the open discussion rather than to shame and judge for the admission is a difficult—but a worthwhile task, indeed.

It would be very difficult to hear of a partner's temptation to talk more with a co-worker than necessary, or hear of a new online friend.

In fact, I can think of few things more difficult.

Certainly, one of the few things more difficult would be to find out a few months later that your spouse has had an innocent relationship blossom into something that is not at all innocent anymore.

"Big picture" thinking is required for the difficult conversation that keeps the close intimacy, even around difficult things, within the marital bond. To know that your partner finds you safe enough to talk to about even such a painful and difficult topic is a *compliment to the relationship* and the spouse—odd but true.

An alternate strategy is to work at an excellent relationship with your spouse, but to have an accountability friend/group (who is a same sex person for a heterosexual person) to report any temptation or difficulties. It is helpful to have one or two people who are committed to being utterly transparent with you and you with them. People with whom you trust and feel safe.

These friends are assigned the task of helping you stay on the path that ultimately you want to be on. They are pro-marriage/pro-long-term-relationship and supportive of your relationship of your spouse and work to help you keep it strong. This means finding not just buddies, but folks who are willing to challenge you and gently walk alongside you during rough spots, saying tough things in a way that inspires you to make wise choices when your brain isn't thinking with its smartest parts. (Sometimes, a pair or group is created where members do this with and for each other.)

This is tough stuff.
To stay faithful in a world that offers temptations as near as a few clicks of a mouse away on online chat rooms, or a marathon project at the office is a challenge.

These conversations are hard to have, even for couples that are used to having them. They may be impossible to have for couples who have never been this vulnerable and candid with each other before.

This is where a professional can help. A therapist can guide you through these conversations so that experiencing a difficult topic like this is something that creates a stronger bond between you, rather than distance and outrage. Professional therapy is very helpful to talk about relationships that are seemingly "just friends" but actually feel sinister and threatening.

These conversations are hard, but worthwhile. The reward of a lifelong earned, fought-for, valued, treasured growing marriage makes it worth it.

10 DOES YOUR MARRIAGE NEED A COMA?

Sometimes, a marriage is in such bad shape, it needs a coma.

A Controlled Separation is to a couple, what a medically induced coma is to a severely injured patient.

***

Let me explain:

Scientific American explained medically induced coma:[xii] it is a state of unconsciousness created by highly trained physicians using medication. It slows the body's metabolism down to allow a brain that is swelling to heal. The coma protects the brain from further damage that could be caused by further swelling.

Medically induced comas are a drastic measure that attempts to save a life. They are used when the injuries are life threatening.

The article also goes on to say that although the medically induced coma is carefully done under the full supervision of physicians with medication used in surgery, there are risks, and an effort is made to make the period of coma as brief as possible.

The subtitle to the article: **Medically induced comas are only**

used when other options are lacking.

In other words, it's a last ditch effort. And when nothing else is working, a medically induced coma can potentially save a person's life.

Not nearly always.

But sometimes.

***

There are times in some marriages where the relationship is so raw that even attempts to save it create further damage.

Times when desperate attempts to fix it are received poorly and make things worse.

Sometimes, the raw reaction to a relationship crisis catches one or both spouses off guard. Yelling, throwing things, saying nasty things that are out of character, waking a spouse up in the middle of the night to ask questions for which there are no good answers. A person may feel powerless to stop, even though it's clear that this isn't helpful. The **collateral damage** creates another whole level of crap to have to work through.

Other times, a person is going through their own internal turmoil that creates distance within the couple. The couple is having trouble connecting, while one spouse is overwhelmed with their own internal suffering. It feels too much to work on themselves as an individual and within the marriage. They can't breathe or think or live one more day like this.

Still other times, the couple has been struggling for years. Distance. Anger. Disappointment. Disengagement. They can't remember how they got here, they only know it can't continue. It's bad, it's been bad for a long time, but there are no bad people here. But there are kids—and calling it quits doesn't feel like an option either.

In these situations, a marriage coma may be just what is needed to stop the damage.

The marriage coma creates an opportunity for:

- Recovery for one or both spouses to better allow the marriage to have a chance. People can do their own individual work steadily and solidly without couple dynamics creating complications.
- The collateral damage stops. No more yelling, throwing things, people saying things that can't be unsaid or unheard. The agony is felt by the individuals, and shared with a therapist or friend, but the marriage isn't frayed by nasty behavior between spouses.
- Sober second thought. Ending a marriage that has lasted for years is a very big deal. Children are affected. So are in laws. So are retirement plans. Mortgages, friends, traditions, Christmas morning, and family weddings--so much is impacted when a marriage dies.

Ending a marriage is a huge decision. Divorce, a decision that will affect you for the rest of your life, is best made calmly from a place of strength, rather than a desperate decision to get out of an intolerable situation.

A Controlled Separation (i.e. marriage coma) is **very** different than a "trial separation" where people feel out what it is like to be single. A trial separation is like an experiment to see if singleness works. A trial separation and a Controlled Separation are **not** the same.

A Controlled Separation is deliberate. It's hard work.

It's a desperate act that says, "We're not going to give up easily. We are not giving into divorce without giving it everything we've got."

It's an opportunity to say: "The marriage we had is over. That wasn't working. Is it possible to get a new and viable marriage to rise out of the ashes?"

It's often recognizing that divorce might be on the table, but it's not rushing to divorce. Divorce is a big decision. A Controlled Separation slows the process down to make a permanent decision with maximum effectiveness.

There are a few basic components of a Controlled Separation. It is best openly discussed, and written down clearly so as to remove fear and improve understanding:

1. A couple figures out how to create that space--renting an apartment, creating space within the house, one spouse living with family/friends
2. Practical matters are negotiated: looking after the children, finances, etc.
3. Contact with each other is negotiated.
   Dating? Therapy? Texting? How much?
4. Intentional work for each spouse is outlined. Reading books? Resting? Therapy? Journaling? Retreats? Getting together with friends? The Controlled Separation
5. A time frame is established.

Sometimes, it is helpful to work with a therapist to outline what a Controlled Separation should look like. Tempers are often running high in the relationship right at a time when cooler heads will be needed. Lee Raffel writes an excellent book, *Should I Stay or Go? How Controlled Separation (CS) Can Save Your Marriage*[xiii], that explains the whole process in detail.

***

Some great shifts *can* happen in a Controlled Separation as there is space for discovery and healing:

- A spouse can realize that she isn't bringing her best self to the relationship because of how she pushes herself so hard in every area of her life...she is harder on herself than anyone else. She knows this because she is just as stressed when she is living apart from him, so she starts to work on the way she relates to herself. She starts to talk to her husband differently, once she begins to live a healthier, less stressed life.

- A spouse might realize that he hasn't taken initiative to create the marriage he wants. He hasn't told her what works for him. He starts to have conversations where he lets her in on what makes him sad and happy and excited and angry. She loves that he is opening up and now doesn't have to guess at what he's thinking.

- A spouse might realize that it's the marriage he hates, not the spouse. The patterns in their lives are killing their relationship. Once removed from the day to day destructive patterns, the underlying love is felt. The patterns start to emerge.

- A spouse, now living alone half time in the house with the children and their schedules, now realizes the unfair distribution of labor before the separation. That spouse is overwhelmed with responsibilities that normally fall to the other. The spouse understands the resentment in a felt way that just wasn't possible during the fights about emptying the dishwasher and laundry folding.

- With the distance created in the separation...not sharing the bed, no obligatory morning pecks, and no evening television together, one has a chance to find the part that misses their spouse, and feels affection and longing that is buried under the anger that is buried under the fear. That part is too easily buried in the everyday nattering and nitpicking of life.

In other words, Controlled Separation creates space for healing, for exploring, for *feeling all the feels* more freely. Sometimes that space allows for new hope to emerge, and the fragile coals of the relationship to reignite into flames that haven't been around for a while.

To be clear, sometimes Controlled Separation leads to growth and clarity that makes divorce the best choice. It can't save a marriage that isn't save-able. Sometimes, the Controlled Separation makes it clear to one or the other that marriage is no longer realistic. But it can save a marriage that might end prematurely because, it feels too painful to stay together in that moment.

***

Insanity: Doing the same thing over and over, expecting different results.

Einstein didn't say it, though many sources say he did. Doesn't matter where it comes from, this much is true: When a marriage is struggling under the weight of:

- regular fights
- squabbles in predictable and painful patterns
- agonizing distance
- excruciating disengagement

...doing the same thing of hanging in there endlessly doesn't make much sense. The fights get worse, the patterns deeper, the distance greater, and the disengagement more impenetrable.

The alternative doesn't have to be:

1. this ugly marriage *or*
2. that painful divorce.

There is a third way. Look for it. Controlled Separation. New marriage. New patterns. New ways of relating together.

Stop the hurting. Allow for healing.

A medically induced coma is a desperate measure to save a patient's life. If a doctor doesn't try it, it would be negligence. Don't we owe our marriages the same opportunity for healing?

Controlled Separation isn't for the faint of heart.

But neither is divorce.

Sometimes, as painful and frightening as it seems, Controlled Separation is a helpful option.

11 DOES YOUR WIFE IMPACT YOUR LIFE?

This chapter gives you language to talk to your husband. Take paragraphs of it and write it in your own hand to give to him. Add in your own words that speak the pain in your heart. Copy these pages him and put a star beside the bits that speak your heart. Highlight the bits that speak the longings of your soul so he can see the parts you need him to know as truth. Heck, hand over this whole thing if you think that's the right thing to do.

This is a direct letter, but it gives an important message in a civil tone, which isn't always easy when you're tired, angry, and hurt.

A direct style is important, but it's also important to phrase your words in a manner that makes them easier to land on and in him, rather than be pushed away. It's not your responsibility to "make him listen"—that's his job. It *is* your responsibility to engage him so that he knows this comes from a place inside of you that wants to reconnect with him.

***

Dear husbands-whose-wives-are-lonely-for-you,

I'm writing this letter to you because I want you to spend the rest of your days with the love of your life. Truly I do. Some of these words may sound harsh, but they are deliberately bold and blunt because the message is so important.

Some of you may recognize yourselves in this letter. Ask your wife how this letter applies to you?

Some of you may have been given a copy of this letter, or it was left on the front seat of your car, or slipped into your laptop case to find. If you are reading this because your wife gave it to you—do me a favor?

Thank her. Seriously, yes—thank her.

Let your wife know she was very brave and very kind to give it to you. Let her know this letter was a lot to digest so you are thanking her, but you won't be able to discuss it further just yet because you need some time to think it through. Let her know that you want this marriage to work as much as she does, and you had no idea how much it wasn't working for her. Let her know that you want to take it seriously and make lasting changes. Mostly let her know you read it, and it matters to you.

This letter isn't going to be easy to read. It may even make you furious, or want to hide, or get drunk or pull away, or get involved in a super big project in the garage or at work or at the community center to avoid the conversations this letter invites. You may be pissed off because of the implications of this letter.

You may have devoted your life to providing her a good life with secure finances and a beautiful house. You may take her on a big vacation once a year. There are lots of signs you can point to, to show you have really tried to give her what you thought was a good life. To get this letter is really going to hurt because all your good intentions won't feel good enough.

Know that I write it because I want you to stay married to the

67

woman of your dreams.

I'm giving you the biggest "heads up" of your life. I'm giving you an opportunity to ensure that your wife isn't slipping away from you unawares.

I'm inviting you to truly and deeply connect with your wife so she experiences you really connecting to her. Being pals and roommates isn't enough. Inviting her into your interests and passions isn't enough.

There may be cues she has given you in the past that invited you to work on your relationship with her. Remember how you have written it off as a cranky mood? Maybe you chalked it up to "that time of the month". Like when she wanted to go on the couples retreat, or buy a book, or engage in a quiz or exercise from the internet. What if I told you that they were brave bids for connection and when you blew the bids off, she felt blown off?

It's now harder for her to do it again. And so she may not say much.

As the two of you raise your kids, and get together with friends, and buy groceries and pay down the mortgage, and just generally live your lives, she is getting farther and farther away from you. Maybe you haven't even noticed.

Some of these women wake up one morning and say, "no more".

First the bad news: The awful truth that research confirms over and over again:

Research indicates that women initiate divorce 69 percent of the time.

Yep, more than 2/3's of divorces are because the wife says, "I'm done". There are lots of articles that speculate about why women are more likely to initiate divorce. Look it up on the internet. Yes,

I'm asking you to do some research. Yes, fuss a little—for the sake of the one you long ago decided to grow old with.

***

Dear husbands-whose-wives-are-lonely-for-you, I'm going to give you my experience of this, from the viewpoint of the therapist's chair. This is harsh but true. I've been doing this for a while, and this has happened over and over again in our office:

We get an email or a phone call from a desperate husband (often first thing in the morning). He says his wife wants to end their marriage. He is shocked and stunned. He loves her and wants to continue the marriage. He is clearly distraught. He wants an appointment today. As soon as possible. He will move heaven and earth to be there.

And he's hoping his wife will come too. They simply have to work this out. He's sure it can be worked out. She's upset, but things can't really be that bad. He doesn't know why she wants it to end, because things have been OK. There should be a way to fix this— as long as she comes. He really really wants her to come.

They come in together. He is incredulous and incredibly upset. She is tired and flat. She says in an even tone:

> "I've tried for years. I've let him know that this isn't working for me. He would get a little more helpful for a few days, but then when I stopped complaining, he would just go back. He would get a little more conversational or affectionate for a few weeks, and then it went back to the way it was.
>
> I can't do this anymore. I believe he wants to change now. I know he thinks it can be different this time. But I'm done. I don't trust the changes he will make now to last. It's too hard to hope he might actually change—I've

hoped before, and then been disappointed. Can't do it anymore. I'm done."

Sometimes, he comes in alone because she has refused. All of a sudden, he can see crystal clear into their history. In the session, he tells an insightful tale of how he gradually stopped being curious about her interests, how his eyes glazed over when she came home excited from something and she wanted to talk. He can see how he stopped getting up from the couch and let her do most of the house management. He's crushed and desperately motivated to sincerely change—but it's looking like he won't get a chance.

Dear husbands-whose-wives-are lonely-for-you, you don't want that to be you, do you?

***

A wife will tell me that she has tried to reach out to you and has been disappointed for years. She has worked to be:

- supportive of your career with late evenings at work by taking over tasks at home
- a cheerleader for you as you pursue your interests while you went away for the weekend or spent money on your latest pursuit
- patient with your fatigue and let you go to bed early while she made the lunches and got ready for the next day. (Did you even know how tired she was?)

She has spent years:

- tolerating your disengagement
- silently enduring your lack of interest and support in her life
- making up for your distance with the kids and making excuses for you

A wife often does a lot to make her husband's life easier without him realizing it. This might mean giving up her own opportunities to be with her friends, compromising her career or interests in ways she wouldn't even have brought up to you, or even just making your favorite suppers often and rarely making hers.

Statistically, she has done a lot more housework than you have. She has learned to not raise the issue; you taught her that it would only lead to a fight. She has just silently been working more hours than you in a day because everyone just expects it.

More than likely, she has gone for pizza when you wanted pizza, or burgers when you wanted burgers. Do you know where she wants to go? When is the last time you want to a restaurant that she liked that you're not really nuts about, but you went because you knew she'd love it? And then she saw that you truly enjoyed the experience of going to *her* restaurant because you got to see the sparkle of delight in her eye.

***

There are a lot of women who are quite unhappy, but are determined to be kind and respectful. She knows that whining and complaining doesn't draw a husband into a closer marriage.

So she tells her husband that something isn't right and she would like to go for counseling, but when the husband refuses, she doesn't know what else to say. So she says nothing.

Your disappointed wife may leave a marriage book on the coffee table or the nightstand for a looooong time, hoping you'll notice and pick it up, because she intuitively knows that you, for sure, are not going to read it if she asks you directly. She may have even highlighted certain passages she is desperate to have you digest— and you walk by the book every day without acknowledgement.

There is distance that you feel from her. Less sex. Maybe no sex at all. For quite a while. You notice and mention it, because you miss it. But you tune out when she tries to tell you of the distance she feels.

And so when her direct and indirect efforts were rebuffed, she gave up and hung in there for as long as she could.

And then one day, she writes a letter and packs a suitcase, saying she's done.

Women tend to file when they are done.

Finished. Finito. So very, very done.

Dear Husband-whose-wife-is-lonely-for-you...don't let this be your wife. Please.

The wife will use the counseling session he now suddenly dragged her to, to explain that there is nothing left in her to work on this marriage. Leaving now is like when the doctor declares the time of death over a patient.

She isn't killing the marriage. **She's acknowledging it is already dead.**

Typically, husbands-whose-wives-are lonely-for-you, only now is when the husband gets that it is truly serious. And he is flooded with all the feelings of love and connection and adoration that he truly has for his wife.

And he is desperate to fix it. He doesn't want to lose her.

Except she's done.

So, dear husbands-whose-wives-are lonely-for-you, I know you don't mean harm to your wife. You don't mean to allow the marriage to die in front of you without you even knowing about it. You don't mean to ignore her. I get that.

It's not intentional.

It's hard to hear from your life partner that she finds you falling short. It's tempting to push painful information away, like pushing away the Brussel sprouts on your plate and just not eating them.

Women are raised to be sensitive to other's emotions. They notice when their husband is upset and take care of it. They know when he needs extra support, and they give it. Wives are really dialed in to being aware of where their partners are at—women are socialized to really notice and be impacted by what other people are going through.

So, husbands-whose-wives-are-lonely-for-you, this is hard stuff. It's quite possible that you weren't raised in our culture to accept influence. You may never have been taught how to figure out how to actually have what your wife is feeling matter to you in ways that have you check in on her, change what time you go on your fishing trip, offer to take over cleaning up the house because you see she's tired, learn to watch some of the movies the way she may have learned to watch yours.

Simply put: Does your wife experience and see by your actions and your words that her feelings, thoughts and behaviors influence you? Does she see you living a life that actively demonstrates she matters to you?

To accept influence from their husbands is as natural as breathing to most wives.

For most men, accepting influence from their wives doesn't come as naturally.

And accepting influence from your wife, according to John Gottman, one of the leading researchers of love, is critically important in reducing your risk of divorce.[xiv]

So, husbands, there is a brief inventory online that can get you thinking about how well you accept your wife's influence. You can find it here: <https://www.gottman.com/blog/weekend-homework-assignment-do-you-and-your-partner-accept-each-others-influence/>

Take it—and take the results sincerely.[xv]

Better yet, when you've had a chance to gather yourself to truly hear her, ask your wife how much she feels like she matters to you. Ask her how much she feels heard and understood, how much she feels you support and care for her. That will be hard. It will take real courage.

I'm warning you—if she has given you this blog post, when she starts talking, the results may be dismal, and will certainly be disheartening. You may unleash the flood gates of pain. Her parched soul that is thirsty for connection may overwhelm you. Your first impulse might be to be angry. You might want to blame her. Can you prepare yourself to hold off on a harsh reaction?

The irony is that, even in the asking, you are telling her that she matters, as long as you listen to her and *give her an experience of being heard.* Listen to her responses; encourage her to say even more hard stuff to you. If you can keep her talking, and if you can write some stuff down, and really hear her—as hard as it will be—it will be an important step in letting her know that she can feel hope.

It will seem strange to let her talk and open up about her frustration, anger, heartbreak and loneliness while just saying, "I want to know more. I didn't know, and thank you now for telling me."

Don't try to fix it. Don't try explaining. It is not the time for explanations or repair—the irony in this is that as you simply hold her pain, the repair has already begun.

***

Dear husbands-whose-wives-are lonely-for-you, get an accurate read from her on your marriage, now, before she tells you so clearly that there is nothing you can do about it.

Please?

I want you to be able to grow old and happy with your wife.

Make my job as a therapist easier? If she asks you to work on your marriage now before she is completely burnt out--please show up? Stick with the process—and you give yourself a fighting chance?

You give your therapist something to work with when you come before your wife is completely done.

12 A LETTER TO POTENTIAL CLIENTS: YEP, THERAPY IS HARD

Whether or not your husband is willing to go to therapy, you may benefit from going to counseling, even if it is alone. It's a chance to learn about yourself, your input into the marriage, and how where you come from shapes your responses to him. Consider counseling for yourself, as a wife whose marriage is struggling.

***

If your husband is willing to consider counseling, then pass this on to him?

***

Hey, if you're reading this, it's because your wife has said the two of you need therapy. It may have come as a calm request. Or maybe a gentle plea.

Or the two of you may be past all that and you're reading because of an ultimatum: Come to couple therapy with me or we're done.

I suspect you've avoided marriage counseling in the past because the whole idea seems foreign to you. Distasteful.

Too *touchy-feely*.

I'll give you that…therapy often does involve talking about feelings.

However, think back to the beginning of your relationship. Did you get married because it only seemed the practical thing to do? Remember the feelings that drove you to decide to spend the rest of your lives together?

And trust me, it is your feelings right now have you resist therapy. The very thing that could save and enrich the most important relationship is something that raises discomfort and unease inside. It is feelings that have kept you out of the therapy room.

Feelings are important. Feelings drive behavior, as inconvenient as that might seem.

You've heard your spouse, and are now considering therapy. Let me talk to you about what therapy is about. You might be surprised.

***

My husband, Jim, and I made a deal with each other when we got married. We promised each other that if either one of us said to the other: "I'd like to go see a therapist", the other will agree to go. No excuses or wiggling out of it.

The idea is that if one of us feels like we need to go to a counselor, it's quite possible it is because one of us is feeling misunderstood or not heard in the relationship. And if that is the case, it would be quite possible that the reason why therapy is felt to be needed wouldn't be understood either. So, the natural tendency would be for one to not see the need to go to therapy at precisely the moment when the reason is very important for the other. Thus, our pre-arranged agreement to agree to go.

Do you know your own blind spots? Of course not! Nobody, by definition, can know their own blind spots.

Jim and I talk regularly about how each of us is feeling in our relationship. If Jim, for some reason, starts to feel like something isn't right, and his attempts to talk to me about it don't go well, I would like to know that he has a means to address it.

Part of loving Jim is ensuring that our marriage is working well for him. And because I know I'm not perfect, I may not only goof up, but then also botch the way I handle it when he tries to tell me about my goof. Our marriage only works well if it is working for both of us. If it isn't working for him, then it's not working for me either.

***

As a person contemplating entering counseling, I feel like there are a few things you need to know. A lot more people have considered counseling than have actually made an appointment. Many people wonder about making an appointment, maybe even want to make an appointment—but don't.

I want to make sure that if you decide to not come to counseling, you are doing it for the right reasons.

I spoke to a friend this week who is in serious crisis. Other friends of ours were encouraging her to make an appointment with a therapist. In the end she spent the money for a session on paint for her bedroom. She spent her spare time for a week making her bedroom into her own little personal haven--a beautiful place to rest when the world feels harsh and confusing. She maintains that this was the best therapy for her.

Good on her for making that decision!

She did some important healing. She did therapy. Just not in an office with a therapist.

Sometimes a new coat of paint truly is therapy.

Go for it—or any other activities/relationships that are truly healing.

But sometimes people who don't go to therapy avoid healing altogether.

That makes me sad.

***

It's hard to know that there might be healing from the hurting for people, and they aren't grabbing the opportunity, and squeezing it.

I love it when people grab an opportunity to heal—whether it is painting the walls of their room, books/movies/workbooks, or therapy—and are careful to squeeze every last drop of healing out of the opportunity into their hearts.

I think there are reasons people choose to not go to counseling for healing. I'm going to invite you to think on these. Decide if you are choosing not to go to counseling for good reasons. These are reasons that I think are powerfully and strongly given, that in my mind, just don't hold up:

1. You've been told counseling is for sissies (or wimps, or weaklings or something of the sort)

Evidently you've never witnessed a counseling session.

Simply put: therapy is one long exercise in vulnerability.

Brené Brown, one of my favorite researchers, says that vulnerability sounds like truth and feels like courage. But it is never weakness. I know that thought to be true.

My clients show me raw courage. Every. Single. Day.

Therapy is hard and risky work. It means:

- Going to places inside and saying things out loud that haven't seen the light of day for years, or maybe ever.
- Acknowledging responsibility for the way things haven't been going well in your marriage.
- Expressing discomfort about your troublesome marriage with a therapist, and then even to your spouse.
- Being real about how fears that have developed from the ghost of trauma past continue to pull the strings in your life.
- Going beneath the anger to acknowledge the fear, or be real about the loss, or to feel the hurt
- Acknowledging the use of old patterns that worked well when you were younger, but now are pulling you out of your authenticity and make it hard for you to show up in your life right now.

Please know that if you show up in a therapy office, you are seen by the therapist as a person who is strong and courageous in being willing to look at the hardest parts of your life.

I see you, as a new client, as a wise investor--willing to do hard things because you believe that the healing inside yourself and in your relationships will be a payoff that is well worth it.

2. You've been told that therapy is all about blaming your mother/father/bully/abuser—and it just seems like that's a lousy use of money

Bad things happen to good people. Life isn't fair. Trauma shapes us powerfully. We don't have to like it. It's just truth.

But healing means taking responsibility for your own internal suffering. It means being aware not only of what happened, but how you tell yourself a story about what happened. It means growing to accept that others are often doing the best they can, even when they are doing bad and hurtful things.

Those insights--when you get them at a soul level; well, that changes a person.

It means drawing boundaries and having hard conversations. It means grieving things that will never be...and then letting go of the dream that will never be.

I'll warn you. Therapy is hard.

Once you start counseling, you won't be able to keep on blaming others for your internal discomfort.

It means looking inside for how your reaction to what has happened shapes your experience of what happened. It's often the story we tell ourselves about what happened that shapes how we see the world. The story we tell ourselves is often an unconscious confabulation where we honestly believe a lie about ourselves or the world.

There is no way to know when we are making up or adding to the data without someone hearing our story and helping us work through it. Perspective is essential...and how are we supposed to see parts of ourselves we can't see?

Pain is inevitable. Suffering is optional.

But trust me, easier said than done.

3. You think it's better to do this alone

A lot of people believed for a long time that the earth was flat.

Even when science said the world was round, folks denied it, and maintained the belief that the earth was a pancake.

They can believe the earth is a giant Frisbee, but that doesn't change the reality: the earth is a giant ball.

We are wired for connection. We need each other. Science is very clear on this.

"I don't need anybody," or "I don't let anybody in," or "I'll only get hurt if I am vulnerable," are all emotional and relational equivalents of, "the world is flat".

We understand the world and ourselves best in community. Therapy is an excellent place to start connecting if you live in a world where you have always believed, "I don't need anybody".

I've had many clients (most often they are men) that tell me within the first 10-15 minutes of an initial session that they have told me more of their inner world than they have told anybody. Ever.

These people who are opening up--for the first time in their lives— they are terrified and second guessing themselves. *They also wonder out why they waited so long.* Once people start the process of hearing themselves think out loud with another person, they recognize its value. It's hard and challenging—and a therapist can't promise you a straight upward line of linear progress.

Talking to another person about the secrets and the fears and the inadequacies of one's life paradoxically feels life-giving and soul-saving. It acts like a glass of clean, cool water to a parched and thirsty soul. The dry cracks start to fill in, even in just the sharing of one's story. It's not only terrifying—it's fantastic!

***

Secrets kill. Therapy is a great place to start speaking out, to practice talking about the things that secretly hijack your life. Once they are spoken of, they lose their power.

Wayne Brady, a comedian speaks of the tremendous pressure that culture puts on people--especially men--to pretend they are OK, even if they are not OK. He has a great video that can help you understand the pressure.[xvi] He invites you to consider giving yourself permission to let somebody in.

***

So, dear-person-who-is-considering-counseling, know that there is a therapist who is ready to explore this with you. Make the call or write the email, and get the work started. Get your brave on, and tell your story to someone who wants to help you write a better story.

You might have some questions about what it is really like to book an appointment. or what to expect the first session. Ask the therapist whatever you need to, to make it possible for you to show up at an appointment.

You don't have to go to counseling if it's not right for you. But please make sure that you're not just making excuses. Please be candid with yourself if you are avoiding something big in your life.

And if you decide to attend a session alone, or with your spouse, know a few things:

- It's extremely common to notice yourself checking for a sore throat, or thinking about scheduling an emergency meeting, or suddenly feeling a lot of pressure to do something else at the precise time the therapy appointment is scheduled. That's normal. Notice your desire to not attend the session, and store it away as valuable information. Talk to the therapist about your reluctance, if you dare. Go anyway.
- The first session is often an opportunity the therapist has to get the picture of your relationship. Your marriage

didn't start to struggle within a day—it's not reasonable to expect huge changes after a single session. Feeling like nothing was fixed within the first session is not a valid reason to stop going. Keep at it for several sessions before you decide.

- Therapy is opening things up; it's creating dialogue where there hasn't been any. If you get angry or scared or upset or feeling blamed, it is because you and your wife are finally talking about something important. Those feelings are uncomfortable, but they aren't information that actually says, "Stop going". Those are feelings that are actually helpful to bring up in therapy.

- Therapy is for both of you. It would be weird if you didn't hear things that are painful. When your wife says she is angry about something that you've done, hear it and be curious. Notice when you are upset, but work to hold your discomfort and keep listening. That won't be easy, but it will tell your wife that you find her thoughts and feelings important. You don't have to agree with them, but I will ask you to work towards understanding where they come from. The understanding is far more important to healing the relationship than if you agree with what she is saying. Listen with your heart, not only your head.

- If the therapist ticks you off, tell him/her. That is important. You are important in therapy, just as your spouse is. If something is said that feels inaccurate or painful, bring it up so that it can be unpacked and processed.

- If, after several sessions, it doesn't feel like it is going anywhere, talk with your therapist about it. If you're going together, talk with your spouse about it. Is it because you are resistant to the process, or because the therapist isn't "synching" with you? It absolutely is really hard to start with another therapist, if the first one doesn't connect with you. But starting with another therapist is not nearly as hard as a divorce.

- If you don't understand what the therapist means, or what your spouse is saying, just say so. Sometimes we use the same words in different ways. Not understanding and saying so shows your strength and security in yourself.

No matter what, going to a therapist, and sticking with it, shows your spouse that you are sincere in wanting to make the marriage one that you both enjoy. It might not be easy or pleasant, but most important and good things in life that we achieve are borne out of struggle.

I wish you well as you work to improve your marriage!

AFTERWORD

This is not the end.

This is the beginning.

The beginning of hard conversations and wise decision making. Making the difficult happen, because if it's almost dead, what do you have to love?

The beginning of remembering your own worth and value as a human being. Of knowing that you are deserving of respect and dignity. That is without question.

The beginning of not settling for something that doesn't work. The beginning of pursuing the connection that you once had so long ago, you almost can't remember. But it was there, long ago.

The beginning of courageous acts that might not be popular, but are deeply and profoundly good.

The beginning of brave utterances that give your husband the chance to hear your voice, your dreams, your boundaries, your passions, and your desires. It's hard to start, but being heard is ultimately always a good thing. Always.

I wish you well. I wish you courage and strength as you negotiate difficult circumstances. I wish you laughter and a sense of humor as you reconnect with your love. I wish you wisdom as you decide when and where and how to make your position clear. I wish you discernment as you figure your unique path forward.

ABOUT THE AUTHOR

Carolyn Klassen is director and therapist at Conexus Counselling, a large, respected and busy private practice in Manitoba, Canada. She has appeared in HuffingtonPost Canada articles and Sun Media national columns. Carolyn is a regular weekly guest on one of Canada's flagship talk radio programs, as well as various other media interviews on radio, television, and print. Carolyn is a dynamic speaker delivering workshops, retreats, and seminars to help people connect more effectively with themselves, others, and The Divine. She writes a blog entitled, "A Thoughtful Look at Life" at <conexuscounselling.ca>. Carolyn is a Certified Daring Way™ facilitator, an experiential process developed out of the research of Dr. Brené Brown.

Carolyn is happily married with a crew of sons and now some daughter-in-laws. She loves café mistos, visiting with friends, and sitting in the bleachers watching her kids play sports.

Carolyn believes we are wired for connection. She has a special interest in removing barriers that stop people from reaching their goals. Live the life and have the connections you were created for!

Notes:

[i] Dr. Michael Rosenfeld from Stanford University has done this research. You can read about it in multiple places, but here is a good place to start:

Robb, A. (2015, August 24) *Why women are more likely than men to initiate divorce*. Retrieved from: http://nytlive.nytimes.com/womenintheworld/2015/08/24/why-women-are-more-likely-than-men-to-initiate-a-divorce/

[ii] Bureau of Labor Statistics. (2016, December 20) *American Time Use Survey*. Retrieved from: https://www.bls.gov/tus/charts/household.htm

[iii] Benson, K. (2016, October 7) *Emotionally Intelligent Husbands Are Key to a Lasting Marriage*. Retrieved from: https://www.gottman.com/blog/emotionally-intelligent-husbands-key-lasting-marriage/

[iv] There are a lot of articles written about Dr. Ronald Rogge's work at the University of Rochester looking at the value of watching and discussing movies as a couple. Solid research that says watching and then discussing the movie reduces divorce rate. See, for example,

Carrol, L. (2014, February 10) *Movie therapy: 8 films that might save your troubled marriage*. Retrieved from: https://www.today.com/health/movie-therapy-8-films-might-save-your-troubled-marriage-2D12074340

[v] I can't recommend Brené Brown's books enough. *Daring Greatly* in particular is about figuring out how to show up and really dare to be real in your life. This quote is from page 51.

Brown, B. (2015). *Daring Greatly: How the Courage to Be Vulnerable*

Transforms the Way We Live, Love, Parent, and Lead. New York: Avery.

[vi] Another great quote from *Daring Greatly,* page 52.

[vii] Dr. Sue Johnson has developed Emotionally Focused Couple Therapy (EFT), a model of couple therapy that has some great research behind it. Her books are great ones for couples to read. There are therapists that are knowledgeable in her approach who carefully work with couples on the bond they have with each other. EFT is a model that specifically looks at connection.
The quote is from her website:

Johnson, S. (2017). *A Quiet Revolution.* Retrieved from: http://www.drsuejohnson.com/love/a-quiet-revolution/

[viii] No author. (2016, June) *Loneliness has same risk as smoking for heart disease.* Retrieved from: https://www.health.harvard.edu/staying-healthy/loneliness-has-same-risk-as-smoking-for-heart-disease

[ix]Dr. Sue Johnson created the idea of A.R.E. and it is a key concept in Emotionally Focused Couple Therapy. You can read lots more about it here:

Johnson, S. (2008). *Hold me Tight: Seven Conversations for a lifetime of Love.* New York: Little, Brown and Company.

For a helpful quiz to further think this through between you and your husband, you might want to look here:

Adamson, S. (2015, September 9). *How emotionally responsive is your partner? Dr. Sue Johnson's A.R.E. Questionnaire.* Retrieved from: https://cmfcdallas.com/2015/09/a-r-e-questionnaire/

[x] Fisher, H. (Speaker) (2008, February) *The brain in love.* (TED talk) United States: TED.

[xi] Helen Glass writes eloquently about "walls and windows" in her book looking at infidelity.

Glass, Helen. (2004). *Not "Just Friends": Rebuilding Trust and Recovering Your Sanity After Infidelity*. New York: Atria Books.

[xii] Biello, D. (2011, January 10). *What is a Medically Induced Coma and Why Is It Used?* Retrieved from: https://www.scientificamerican.com/article/what-is-a-medically-induced-coma/

[xiii] Raffel, L. (1999) *Should I Stay or Go? How Controlled Separation (CS) Can Save Your Marriage*. New York: McGraw Hill.

[xiv] Pincus, J. (2017, July 31*). Husbands Can Only Be Influential if They Accept Influence*. Retrieved from: https://www.gottman.com/blog/husband-can-influential-accept-influence/

[xv] This is meant to start a discussion and raise awareness...not give you a score that is the final judgement of your ability to be a husband:

Lisitsa, E. (No Date). *Weekend Homework Assignment: Do You and Your Partner Accept Each Other's Influence?* Retrieved from: https://www.gottman.com/blog/weekend-homework-assignment-do-you-and-your-partner-accept-each-others-influence/

[xvi] Brady, W. (2015, January 21). *#StrongerThanStigma - Wayne Brady: Why I Waited to Talk About My Depression*. Retrieved from: https://www.youtube.com/watch?v=KFnwJg_4uwM

www.ingramcontent.com/pod-product-compliance
Lightning Source LLC
LaVergne TN
LVHW021539080426

835509LV00019B/2741